GRASSLAND
LIFE CONNECTIONS

T0011455

By Raymond Bergin

BEARPORT
PUBLISHING

Minneapolis, Minnesota

Credits

Cover and title page, © Mark Kostich/iStock, © KenWiedemann/iStock, © Anagramm/ iStock, © Somchai Sookkasem/iStock, © Krasowit/Shutterstock, © alslutsky/Shutterstock, © Artiste2d3d/Shutterstock; 4–5, © narvikk/Getty Images; 6–7, © R.M. Nunes/iStock; 9 Top, © Niklas Juritsch/iStock; 9 Bottom, © brytta/iStock; 10, © Steve watkins/iStock; 10–11, © Simon Kovacic/Alamy; 12–13, © Eugene R Thieszen/Shutterstock; 14–15, © Jonathan/Adobe Stock; 16, © bluegame/iStock; 16–17, © allou/iStock; 18–19, © Jen Watson/Shutterstock; 20–21, © Anand RJ /Alamy; 22–23, © GomezDavid/Getty Images; 24–25, © egon69/iStock; 25, © MirekKijewski/iStock; 26–27, © All Canada Photos/Alamy; 27, © Henk Bogaard/ Shutterstock; 28, © takahashi__kei/iStock; 29 step 1, © kakteen/Shutterstock; 29 step 2, © Dmytro Zinkevych/Shutterstock; 29 step 3, © wavebreakmedia/Shutterstock; 29 step 4, © Monkey Business Images/Shutterstock; 29 step 5, © eggeegg/Shutterstock.

Bearport Publishing Company Product Development Team
President: Jen Jenson; Director of Product Development: Spencer Brinker; Senior Editor: Allison Juda; Editor: Charly Haley; Associate Editor: Naomi Reich; Senior Designer: Colin O'Dea; Associate Designer: Elena Klinkner; Associate Designer: Kayla Eggert; Product Development Assistant: Anita Stasson

Library of Congress Cataloging-in-Publication Data

Names: Bergin, Raymond, 1968- author.
Title: Grassland life connections / by Raymond Bergin.
Description: Minneapolis, Minnesota : Bearport Publishing Company, [2023] | Series: Life on Earth! Biodiversity explained | Includes bibliographical references and index.
Identifiers: LCCN 2022035350 (print) | LCCN 2022035351 (ebook) | ISBN 9798885094115 (library binding) | ISBN 9798885095334 (paperback) | ISBN 9798885096485 (ebook)
Subjects: LCSH: Grasslands--Juvenile literature. | Grassland ecology--Juvenile literature. | BIodiversity--Juvenile literature.
Classification: LCC QH87.7 .B47 2023 (print) | LCC QH87.7 (ebook) | DDC 333.74--dc23/eng/20220831
LC record available at https://lccn.loc.gov/2022035350
LC ebook record available at https://lccn.loc.gov/2022035351

For more information, write to Bearport Publishing, 5357 Penn Avenue South, Minneapolis, MN 55419.

Contents

A Home Made of Grass

In the middle of a huge, flat field, wildflowers attract birds and bees. Wildebeest, zebras, and buffalo munch on tall grass while a lion roars in the distance. Overhead, vultures fly in circles around the remains of a gazelle the lion has recently killed.

The grasses in grasslands can grow up to 7 feet (2 m) tall. All that grass feeds 25 **species** of large plant-eaters, including buffalo and elephants.

This grassland is bursting with life. But nearby, dust blows across a dry plowed field. Herds of cattle from a farm trample and eat the wild grass, leaving empty patches across the land. What's happening to life on Earth?

A Planet Full of Life

Earth is covered in many **biomes**—areas of land and sea where the **climate** and natural features are a perfect fit for certain kinds of plants and animals. Deserts, forests, tundras, wetlands, oceans, and grasslands are all biomes.

Every biome is home to a connected community of life. This wide variety of connected life is called **biodiversity**. Each grassland biome can include everything from tiny beetles to towering giraffes.

The biodiversity of some grasslands can be packed into small areas. Researchers found that just 1 sq ft (930 sq cm) of a Romanian grassland included 43 different kinds of plants!

What Is a Grassland?

All that life takes up a lot of space. Grasslands cover more than a third of Earth's land. As the name suggests, grasslands are mostly grass. They are not all the same, however.

Savanna grasslands are warm year-round. A rainy season about six to eight months long allows a small number of trees and shrubs to grow. This is followed by a very dry period. Temperate grasslands, on the other hand, have hot summers and cold winters. They get less rain than savannas, and there are almost no trees or shrubs.

Lawns, playing fields, golf courses, and grassy public parks are all considered urban grasslands. Their grasses and wildflowers provide shelter and food for many insects, birds, and mammals.

Temperate grassland

Savanna grassland

9

It All Fits Together

All living things within a grassland are important to the survival of the rest. Small plants and creatures in the ground break up hard soil, allowing plant roots to spread and draw up water and **nutrients**. Insects and small rodents find shelter in the plants—and in return they help spread the plants' pollen and seeds. Larger herbivores munch away older plants, making room for new growth. And grassland **predators** hunt those **grazers**, preventing too much grass from being eaten.

Grazers, such as hippos, bison, and horses, are good grassland helpers. As they munch, they push insects out of the grass. Then, egrets swoop in and feast on the bugs.

The Importance of Fire

All the life in grasslands also depends upon one surprising thing for survival—fire! Natural grassland fires are often started by lightning sparking dry-season grasses. The fires do not burn super hot because there isn't much woody plant material to fuel them. So, the soil stays cool enough that plant roots remain unharmed. Some small creatures can wait out the fires underground. Larger animals can outrun the relatively slow-moving flames.

What's left in the fires' wake supports new life. Wildfire ash **fertilizes** the soil and new grasses can grow as much as 1 inch (2.5 cm) per day. Animals that eat the plants have plenty of food.

During wildfires, birds chow down on the insects, mice, and lizards that are driven out of hiding by the flames.

Unhindered, grassland fires may spark every year or two. This makes the soil rich for the next growing season.

Dangerously Dry

Life in grasslands thrives due to a delicate balance of rainy periods followed by dry spells and regular fires. But what happens if this balance is thrown off? We're starting to see. Grassland biomes are harmed as our planet warms up. They are experiencing hotter and drier weather, with less rainfall. This can lead to **droughts** that result in the death of grasses and other plants.

When grasses and flowers disappear, pollinators soon follow. Grazing animals lose their food and shelter, so they must relocate, too. Larger predators go hungry as the complex food web collapses.

Whenever we burn fuel to power our cars, homes, and factories, we add a heat-trapping gas called **carbon dioxide** to the **atmosphere**. As a result, our planet is warming up.

Farm Harm

Humans are also taking over grassland biomes. The rich soil in healthy grasslands is too tempting for many farmers to pass up. They plant crops where grasses and wildflowers used to be. Hundreds of plant species are suddenly replaced by only one or two kinds of plants.

Single-crop fields do not provide food and shelter to nearly as many animals and insects. Birds are having an especially hard time with this loss of biodiversity. In the last half century, more than 50 percent of grassland birds have left or died off.

Without plant biodiversity, soil loses nutrients. The beetles and spiders that kill plant pests die. So, farmers need to use fertilizers and **pesticides** on their crops, harming even more plants and animals.

A lack of plant biodiversity on farms soon leads to a loss of animal diversity, too.

Too Much Munching

Much like farmers, ranchers also look at grasslands and see them as the perfect place for their hungry cattle, sheep, and goats. Herds of **livestock** eat grassland plants. What doesn't end up in their stomachs ends up under their hooves. Herds trample and destroy many of the remaining plants.

As ranches take over the land, grassland plants and soil are not given enough time to bounce back and create new, healthy growth. Large areas become empty, leaving grassland wildlife hungry and without a home. When the grasses die, so does all the life they support.

When grassland soil is trampled, it gets packed down, and grasses cannot regrow. Bare soil is then carried away by wind and water, leaving the land **barren**. After this happens, future growth is nearly impossible.

Lost in the Woods

Even when we're trying to do good for the planet, we sometimes wind up harming grasslands. Because trees remove a lot of heat-trapping carbon dioxide from the atmosphere, people are planting them in or near grasslands.

However, thirsty trees reduce the flow of streams and rivers within grasslands, drying them out. The shade trees create kills off flowering plants and pushes out animals that need open spaces and direct sunlight. Soon, forests squeeze out grasslands—and all of the plant and animal life in them.

Tree shade kills grasses and plants that zebras, antelope, and other grazers eat. Lions hiding behind trees and tall shrubs more easily sneak up on these grazers.

Fighting Fires, Killing Grasslands

To protect the farms, ranches, and planted forests that have spread into grasslands, people are no longer letting natural wildfires burn. But without fire, grasslands die.

When grassland fires are put out immediately, the soil becomes less rich. Without occasional fires to clear them out, trees and tall shrubs can take root and steal water and sunlight from **native** plants. Dead plant material is not burned, so there is less space and light for the new, nutritious plant life that grassland wildlife depends upon for food.

Without regular fires, the dry, woody underbrush becomes more of a fire hazard. When they do eventually spark, wildfires often burn through dried plants faster and hotter than they would through a typical grassland.

People and Grasslands

If grasslands become unhealthy, so will we. For one thing, grasslands keep our planet cool! Their soil stores up to a third of the world's heat-trapping carbon. The soil and grasses' light color also reflects warming sunlight back up to the sky.

Our food supply depends upon the hundreds of thousands of grassland animals—including bats, bees, flies, moths, beetles, birds, and butterflies— that spread seeds and pollinate food crops. Vitamin- and mineral-rich grasses and hay feed our livestock, which, in turn, provide us with nourishing meat and milk.

Many of the 800 million people who live in grasslands burn grasses in cooking fires and to heat their homes—homes that often have walls and roofs made of grassland thatch.

Grassland Life Returns

All around the world, people are taking steps to protect grasslands. In many cases, this means managing grasslands in a way that lets nature take the lead.

Some ranchers now keep their livestock moving when grazing, similar to how wild grazers feed in different places. This prevents large areas from being stripped of life and allows grasses to regrow. More natural fires are allowed to burn and controlled fires are set to keep shady trees in check, nourish the soil, and encourage native grasses and flowering plants to grow. Efforts like these are preserving the biodiversity of life in the grasslands.

Some farmers and ranchers are using fewer pesticides, allowing beetles to naturally fight off harmful plant pests. Dung beetles can then do their thing—bury other animals' poop to fertilize grassland soil.

Save the Grassland

What can we do to save our gorgeous grasslands? If we join in their protection and reduce the amount of heat-trapping carbon dioxide we create, we can take a step in the right direction.

If you have a lawn, consider turning part of it into a mini-grassland! Plant native grasses and flowers to provide food and shelter for birds, bees, insects, and other little creatures.

If you live in an area that is trying to restore a local prairie or meadow, join in the cleanup and planting effort.

Ask your school to consider planting native plants and putting up bird houses.

Avoid burning fuel and using gas whenever possible. If possible and safe, walk, ride a bike, or take public transportation to get where you're going.

Electricity is often made by burning fuel. Save electricity by turning off lights when you're not using them, keeping your heat set low, and unplugging all devices when not in use.

Glossary

atmosphere a layer of gases that surrounds Earth

barren unable to grow plants

biodiversity the existence of many different kinds of plants and animals in an environment

biomes regions with a particular climate and environment where certain kinds of plants and animals live

carbon dioxide a gas given off when fossil fuels are burned

climate the typical weather in a place

droughts long periods of time during which there is very little or no rain

fertilizes adds nutrients to soil that make it easier for plants and trees to grow

grazers animals that feed on plant and tree material

livestock animals raised on farms or ranches, such as cows, sheep, and goats

native originally belonging to a certain place

nutrients vitamins, minerals, and other substances needed by living things for health and growth

pesticides chemicals that kill insects and other pests that damage crops

predators animals that kill and eat other animals

species groups that animals and plants are divided into according to similar characteristics

Read More

Bergin, Raymond. *Fires Everywhere (What on Earth? Climate Change Explained).* Minneapolis: Bearport Publishing, 2022.

Cocca, Lisa Colozza. *Grassland Animals (Biome Beasts).* North Mankato, MN: Rourke Educational Media, 2020.

Howell, Izzi. *Biodiversity Eco Facts (Eco Facts).* New York: Crabtree Publishing Co., 2019.

Latham, Donna. *Biomes: Discover the Earth's Ecosystems with Environmental Science Activities for Kids (Build it Yourself).* White River Junction, VT: Nomad Press, 2019.

Learn More Online

1. Go to **www.factsurfer.com** or scan the QR code below.
2. Enter "**Grassland Connections**" into the search box.
3. Click on the cover of this book to see a list of websites.

Index

About the Author

Raymond Bergin lives in New Jersey. Though it is the most densely human-populated state in the country, it remains one of the country's most biodiverse regions. One of Bergin's favorite local hiking spots is a grassland preserve that is home to grasses, wildflowers, and sensitive animal species.

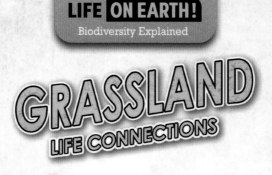

LIFE ON EARTH!
Biodiversity Explained

GRASSLAND
LIFE CONNECTIONS

Grassy growth is being trampled, and birds are flying away never to return. The plants and animals in grasslands depend on one another for survival. What is happening to life on Earth? Discover all about biodiversity and its importance to grasslands and to us. Then, learn what you can do to help.

Read all the books in this series:

BEARPORT
PUBLISHING

BearportPublishing.com

ISBN-13: 979-8-88509-533-4

90000

9 798885 095334